THE SUCCEEDING AT INTERVIEWS POCKETBOOK

By Peter English

Drawings by Phil Hailstone

"A practical, easy-to-read guide that debunks some of the myths about selection processes. Reading it will guarantee all candidates a better chance of success!"
Marita Brown, National Programme Lead, Graduate Schemes, NHS Leadership Centre

"After reading this book the challenge will be knowing which jobs to turn down!"
Octavius Black, Managing Director, The Mind Gym

Published by:
Management Pocketbooks Ltd
Laurel House, Station Approach, Alresford, Hants SO24 9JH, U.K.
Tel: +44 (0)1962 735573 Fax: +44 (0)1962 733637
E-mail: sales@pocketbook.co.uk
Website: www.pocketbook.co.uk

This edition published 2004. Reprinted 2005, 2007.

British Library Cataloguing-in-Publication Data – A catalogue record for this book is available from the British Library.

ISBN 978 1 903776 07 0

Design, typesetting and graphics by **efex ltd**. Printed in U.K.

CONTENTS

INTRODUCTION

INTERVIEWS: MYTHS & REALITY

This book tells you how to be the best candidate – how to impress good interviewers and how to handle bad interviewers.

It also tells you how to perform well at assessment centres, which are being used increasingly by employers.

Here are some common myths about interviews:

- Interviews are fair and objective
- The job always goes to the best candidate
- Some people are naturally good at interviews, others aren't; it's not something you can change

INTERVIEWS: MYTHS & REALITY

This is the reality:

- Interviews are often a lottery. Lots of research shows that interviewers consistently misjudge how good the candidate will be when they actually start doing the job
- The job usually goes to the person who performs best at the interview. Often they aren't the best person for the job. Some people are particularly good at impressing interviewers
- Everyone can get better, a lot better. All it takes is preparation and practice, and this book tells you how

WHAT DO INTERVIEWERS LOOK FOR?

Bad interviewers and good interviewers look for different things.

Bad interviewers:

- Judge you on your performance in the interview
- Place undue emphasis on confidence, appearance and body language
- Rely on their gut feelings when making a decision
- Are unaware of their prejudices
- Act as amateur psychologists, analysing your behaviour too deeply
- May try to trip you up with trick questions
- Are strongly influenced by whether or not they like you
- May play on your nervousness and try to make you feel uncomfortable
- Want to catch you out

WHAT DO INTERVIEWERS LOOK FOR?

Good interviewers:

- Are primarily interested in whether you will be competent in the job
- Try not to be unduly influenced by their personal tastes and preferences
- Will take notes during the interview so they can base their decision on information about your experience and achievements, rather than their subjective impression of how you came across
- Will use ratings scales to score you
- Base their questions solely on the job requirements
- Understand that you will be nervous and try to put you at your ease
- Want to see the best of you

This pocketbook tells you how to impress both types of interviewer.

NOTES

HOW TO BE THE BEST-PREPARED CANDIDATE

PREPARATION THAT EVERYONE WILL DO

This says to the panel: *'I'm as good as the other candidates'.*

Look closely at any information they have sent you, including:

- Person specification (ie, the list of qualities that they are looking for)
- Job description
- Organisational structure charts
- Information about the organisation
- Information about the selection process

Don't forget to look at the organisation's website.

PREPARATION THAT GIVES YOU THE EDGE

This says to the panel: *'I'm really serious about this job'*. It gives you the edge over the other candidates (because they may not have thought to do it).

1. Read between the lines

Read between the lines of the information they have sent you, and see if that tells you anything about the job that is not explicit in the advertisement or the information pack.

They say the job is a new position and that they are looking for self-starters. This suggests that the duties may be a bit unstructured for a while, so you should present yourself as someone who is comfortable working in an environment where things are changing quickly.

2. Phone a friend

Use your network to try and find a friend of a friend who works in the organisation and can give you the insider's view of what it's like working there.

This can be a lot more informative, and easier to digest, than trying to make sense of the organisation's annual report.

PREPARATION THAT GIVES YOU THE EDGE

3. Find out who will be there

Telephone the Human Resources Department and find out who is on the interview panel.

It always helps to know this, and it can also alert you to some of the key relationships in the job.

You are applying for the post of Head of Customer Services and you discover that one of the people on the interview panel will be the Head of Customer Relations. The existence of this person may come as a surprise and you may well want to ask how the two roles relate to one another.

You will also want to use the interview to get an idea of whether the Head of Customer Relations is someone that you would feel comfortable working with.

PREPARATION THAT GIVES YOU THE EDGE

4. Practise

Practise any tests that you will have to undertake as part of the selection process.

Ways of practising in advance include:

- Looking at the internet site **http://www.shl.com**. This gives you the chance to practise some of the most commonly used psychometric tests. However, it's important to be aware that the practice tests on the website may be a lot easier than the ones you will face in a real selection situation.
- Trying the tests and quizzes in 'Test Your IQ' books.

Rehearse any formal presentation until you are word perfect. Don't use notes. If you can present using just your overheads as a prompt, you will appear much more polished and confident than the other candidates.

PREPARATION THAT GIVES YOU THE EDGE

5. Know why you are right for the job

It's really important **to be clear in your own mind** about the knowledge, skills and personal qualities that you possess and that make you the right person for the job. Everything else: confidence, good interview answers, strong body language, follows from this.

Men are from Mars, women are from Venus
It is said that if a man looks at a person specification and finds that he has five of the six qualities that the employer is looking for, he says to himself, *'I'll probably be offered the job'.*

If a woman looks at a person specification and finds that she has five of the six qualities that the employer is looking for, she says to herself, *'I don't have everything they are looking for so it's not worth applying'.*

In this situation it's better to adopt the male approach, because it's quite unusual for a candidate to meet completely every single one of the essential and desirable criteria that the employer has listed on their specification.

PREPARATION THAT GIVES YOU THE EDGE

6. Know what you want to show the panel

One of the worst feelings is to come out of an interview knowing that the interviewers didn't get to see your true abilities.

Sometimes it's because they didn't ask the right questions. However, if you want to be the candidate with an edge over the others, **you have to be able to get your points over even if the panel aren't asking you the 'right' questions.**

There are three steps to making sure that the interview panel find out about your abilities:

Step 1: **Identify** your key strengths in relation to the job they are offering

Step 2: **Prepare** stories and examples that illustrate your strengths

Step 3: **Rehearse** talking about your stories and examples

PREPARATION THAT GIVES YOU THE EDGE

STEP 1: IDENTIFY

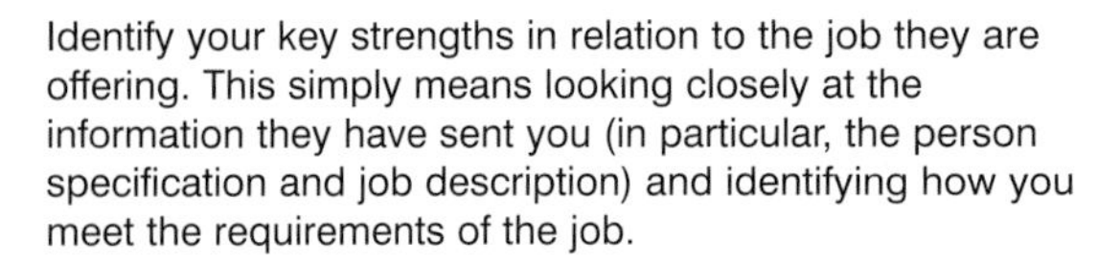

Identify your key strengths in relation to the job they are offering. This simply means looking closely at the information they have sent you (in particular, the person specification and job description) and identifying how you meet the requirements of the job.

Don't forget to draw on your experience outside work.

If it's clear that they are looking for someone who can show initiative and be determined, you could, for example, present experiences gained through travel overseas as strong evidence of these qualities.

PREPARATION THAT GIVES YOU THE EDGE

STEP 2: PREPARE

Prepare some stories and examples. Having stories and examples is absolutely vital if you want to come across as a candidate with some depth of experience.

The formula to follow for each story or example is:

First Sentence: Describe what the problem was
Second Sentence: Describe what you did
Third Sentence: Describe the outcome

'When I moved into my current post we had big problems in our relationships with suppliers. (The problem)

I set up a schedule of regular meetings with each supplier with the aim of improving communications. (What you did)

We now have much better relationships and far fewer problems with deliveries.' (The outcome)

PREPARATION THAT GIVES YOU THE EDGE

STEP 3: REHEARSE

Rehearse, rehearse, rehearse.

Why?
Rehearsing how you will talk about your examples is crucial. Interviews are often stressful and **when under stress we can be less articulate than normal**. The points you could make confidently and fluently with your friends in the pub won't come to your lips as easily when your palms are sweating and your heart is thumping.

How?
Practise describing your examples out loud. This is important because it will:

- Help you get used to telling your stories
- Enable you to test out the exact phrases you want to use

WHAT (NOT) TO WEAR

Rule 1 **Be smart.** Some interviewers will draw all sorts of conclusions about you from the fact that your shoes aren't polished. Smartness means different things in different organisations (see Rule 2).

Rule 2 **Fit in.** Interviewers will be asking themselves (perhaps unconsciously), *'Would this person fit in?'* Their answer to this question will depend partly on what you wear. In some organisations everyone wears a smart suit; other companies are more casual. So, if at all possible, hang around outside the building a week or so before the interview, at the beginning or end of the day, to see what people wear to work.

Rule 3 **Be comfortable.** There's nothing worse than wearing a new suit/shirt/blouse that is uncomfortable or just doesn't feel right. Only wear clothes you feel good in for interviews.

GETTING TO THE VENUE

Do a dummy run

Interviewers take a very dim view of candidates who arrive late, so it's best to do a trial run of your journey to the interview venue. If your appointment is at 9 am make sure your dummy run is at the same time – the journey will take longer in rush hour.

Find a coffee shop (NOT a pub)

When you do your dummy run look out for a nearby coffee shop, so you have somewhere to pass the time if you arrive early. (Some interviewers will be irritated if you show up half an hour before your interview.) Don't make the mistake of going into a nearby pub – you'll come out smelling of cigarettes and alcohol even if you've been sipping a lemonade.

AT THE VENUE

Be nice to the receptionist
Sometimes the interviewers will ask the receptionist for his or her views of each candidate. Sometimes the receptionist will find a way of making them known anyway (*'That bloke in the grey suit was a bit rude'*). So treat the reception staff as if they were part of the interview panel.

Visit the cloakroom beforehand
Not just for the obvious reasons, but also to check your appearance. Do your hair and make-up look like they did when you set out? Is your tie hanging where it should be (and has not been blown over your shoulder, unnoticed)?

THE HOLLYWOOD ATTITUDE

The actor George Clooney reckons that in Hollywood there are a lot of actors who go into auditions giving off a faint whiff of desperation: they are over-eager to get the part. Invariably, according to Clooney, the part gets offered to the actor who walks into the room with the attitude: *'I'm great. You need me more than I need you'*.

It's the same with job interviews. Have you ever heard a friend say, *'I went for a job which I didn't want. I was very relaxed at the interview and they ended up offering me the position.'*?

To help you develop the right attitude, think about the following:

- **The interviewers may well be nervous too** – many employers live in fear of appointing someone who turns out to be poor at the job
- **If you have read this pocketbook and applied the tips you will be better prepared for the interview than the vast majority of candidates**

CONTROLLING YOUR NERVES

The first thing to remember is that **just about everyone gets nervous** before a job interview, and that includes the candidates you are competing against.

Remember also that **you feel more nervous than you look**. The interviewers can't see your heart thumping or your stomach churning. You may feel you are blushing or perspiring more than usual, but the vast majority of interviewers simply won't notice.

Interestingly, some interviewers **like a candidate who is a little nervous:** it shows that the candidate is taking the interview seriously.

CONTROLLING YOUR NERVES

Before the interview, try the following:

- Breathe in deeply through your nose, counting to 10. Then exhale through your mouth while counting to 10. Repeat for one minute, concentrating on relaxing your neck and shoulders. You can do this on the bus or train, or while sitting in your car.
- Try humming to loosen up your voice, or yawning in an exaggerated way to relax your facial muscles. You can do this while walking to the building where the interview is being held.
- To relax your shoulder muscles: make a fist, hold it, then relax.

Some candidates find it helpful to view the interview as a **meeting where they have equal status to the interviewer**. Other candidates imagine that they are at a social occasion and **their aim is to be charming and put the other people (ie the interviewers) at their ease**.

IN THE INTERVIEW

IN THE INTERVIEW

MAKING AN ENTRANCE

THREE THINGS TO DO

Studies show that candidates who do three specific things when they enter the room at the start of the interview are scored more highly, on average, than candidates who don't. These three things are:

1. **Smiling**
2. **Making eye contact with the interviewers**
3. **Shaking hands**

MAKING AN ENTRANCE

WHY DO THESE THINGS MATTER?

- **Many interviewers make up their minds about a candidate in the first minute or so of the interview.** They then spend the rest of the interview looking for evidence to support their initial judgement. This is called **the horns/halo effect.** (It's as if the candidate who starts badly sprouts horns like a devil, and then can do nothing right in the panel's eyes, whereas a halo seems to appear above the head of the candidate who starts well.)
- Smiling says, *'I'm confident'* and *'I'm pleased to be here'*. Most panels want to see these attitudes. **Deliberately having a smile on your face also prevents you from walking in with an anxious expression.**
- **Making eye contact demonstrates confidence**, starts to create a feeling of warmth between you and the panel, and prevents you being seen as shifty.

MAKING AN ENTRANCE

GETTING THE HANDSHAKE RIGHT

- Shaking hands can be problematic. It is possible to over-do it by bounding into the room and thrusting your hand, martial arts fashion, towards the startled interviewers.
- It's better simply to **raise your hand slightly** from your side as you walk towards the panel members. Hopefully, if they pick up the cue they will shake your hand. If they don't, you can let your hand fall back unnoticed.
- One thing to remember is that, if you are carrying anything, you should **hold it in your left hand** to leave your right hand free for shaking. This avoids any awkward shuffling of handbags/files/briefcases from hand to hand.
- Practise shaking hands with your friends and family, and then ask them for feedback. Make sure you aren't using the limp *wet fish* shake or *the bonecrusher.*

BODY LANGUAGE

BE YOURSELF

Your body language matters. The interviewers who like to play ‘amateur psychologist’ will be scrutinising you closely. Other interviewers will be influenced by it, perhaps unconsciously.

The trick in interviews is to **be yourself as much as possible.** This is because when you are being yourself you are at your most fluent and articulate. You probably have no trouble putting your views across when you are chatting with your friends.

IN THE INTERVIEW

BODY LANGUAGE

SET YOUR HANDS FREE

Being yourself in an interview means using your hands naturally.

Some people advocate keeping your hands under control in order to look cool, calm and composed. **This is a mistake** because, in reality, it can make you look stilted and wooden.

What's more, having to remember to control your hands becomes one more thing that your overloaded brain has to worry about in the interview. Very few people have obviously intrusive mannerisms, so free up your hands.

IN THE INTERVIEW

BODY LANGUAGE

DON'T BECOME A CHILD

When people are nervous, particularly in situations where they feel the other people in the room are more powerful than them, they might well adopt 'the child pose'.

This is when you sit with your knees together, feet parallel and perhaps tucked under the chair. Your hands are in your lap and your head is slightly down. Your shoulders lean forward and in. The impression is of a polite and submissive child being told off.

One of the reasons you might adopt this pose in a pressurised, formal situation is that you may start by sitting in a position very similar to the child pose, politely, feet and knees together, hands in lap. **This can look formal, but it doesn't take much to slip from this position into the child pose if you feel anxious.**

IN THE INTERVIEW

BODY LANGUAGE

POSTURE

Cross your legs
One way of avoiding the child pose is to sit with one leg crossed over the other at the knee, with hands resting on your leg. If you sit upright and well back in your chair in this position, you will look confident and professional.

Keep your hands off the table
Generally, it is not a good idea to lean on the table or to put your hands across it. The interview panel may feel that you are invading their space.

Tea? Coffee? Water?
It is usually best politely to decline drinks involving cups and saucers – if you're nervous there is too much scope for crockery rattling and spillages. However, a glass of water might be helpful if you have a dry throat.

IN THE INTERVIEW

BODY LANGUAGE

SHARE YOUR EYE CONTACT AROUND

1. **The situation** – It often happens that one member of the interview panel appears friendlier than the others. This is rarely a conscious good cop/bad cop ploy on their part, but you still need to be careful about how you react.

2. **Your likely reaction** – The natural human response, particularly in a stressful situation like an interview, is to make eye contact with people who seem interested in you.

3. **The result** – If you are not careful, you can find yourself directing all your answers at the kindly-faced panel member who made the mistake of giving you an encouraging smile as you stumbled through your first answer. Before long, you will be clinging to the Kindly Interviewer's gaze like a non-swimmer to a rubber ring, making him or her feel uncomfortable, and the other panel members feel snubbed.

4. **The solution** – Share your eye contact around. When asked a question, you should initially reply to the person who posed the question. If your answer is quite long, then it's OK to look at the other interviewers as you continue.

INTERVIEWER'S BODY LANGUAGE

Watch the interviewer's body language.

- In particular, watch for cues from the interviewer about how long you should talk for when answering each question
- If the interviewer is nodding rapidly and saying *'uh huh'*, or starting to have a glazed look in their eyes, it probably means you have said enough
- If the interviewer repeatedly says things like, *'Could you say a bit more about that?'*, then your answers are probably too brief

ANSWERING THE QUESTIONS

THE GOLDEN RULE

The golden rule of being interviewed is that you should treat each question as an opportunity to give the interview panel a concrete example of why you are right for the job.

In practice this means:

- Using the **stories and examples** that you prepared before the interview (see page 19 for the problem/what you did/the outcome formula)
- **Spotting opportunities** to talk about your examples

ANSWERING THE QUESTIONS

REPETITION

'Could you repeat the question, please?'

- Many candidates feel awkward about asking interviewers to repeat the question. You shouldn't – it is very common for a candidate to ask an interviewer to repeat, or elaborate on, a question.
- It only becomes a problem if you have to do so more than once or twice during the interview.
- One major UK employer actually **gives higher interview scores to candidates who ask interviewers to clarify a question.** This is because they believe it demonstrates good active listening skills on the part of the candidate.

IN THE INTERVIEW

ANSWERING THE QUESTIONS

SPOTTING OPPORTUNITIES

How would you answer each of the following questions in a positive way that illustrates one of your key points about your experience and achievements?

'Tell us about your current job'

'How would you handle a difficult colleague?'

'What would you say your strengths are?'

'What weaknesses do you have?'

'Why do you want this job?'

ANSWERING THE QUESTIONS

CURRENT JOB

Pitfalls

The danger is that because you haven't yet settled into the interview you will give a hurried or waffly answer which involves listing all your duties, tailing off as you struggle to remember points 24 and 25 on the third page of your job description.

Note that this question will often be asked early in the interview. Because of the horns/halo effect it is important to have a strong answer prepared and rehearsed.

ANSWERING THE QUESTIONS

CURRENT JOB

'Tell us about your current job'

How to answer this question

Avoid simply listing every aspect of your job. Remember, your aim in the interview is to sell yourself and let the panel know about your strengths.

Give one sentence which summarises your role:

'I manage the accounts team.'

Then go on to talk about one of the stories or examples that illustrates one of your strengths:

'One of the things I've really liked about the job is that I've been able to raise the profile of the accounts team so that we are seen as more than just number crunchers. We used to be a bit of a backwater within the organisation, but now we get invited to contribute to a whole range of initiatives.'

ANSWERING THE QUESTIONS

STRENGTHS

'What would you say your strengths are?'

Pitfalls

There are two traps to avoid here:

1. Feeling uncomfortable about *blowing your own trumpet* and, as a result, giving a half-hearted answer:

   'I suppose I'm quite good at organising myself.'

2. Giving a lot of opinions about yourself without any supporting evidence:

   'I'm really good at getting on with people, I'm extremely well organised, very reliable and a real self-starter.'

ANSWERING THE QUESTIONS

STRENGTHS

'What would you say your strengths are?'

How to answer this question

- It's good to have **three strengths** you can talk about confidently
- The trick is to focus your answer on qualities that you know are **crucial to the job**, and to give evidence in support of your answer

'I believe I have three particular strengths: firstly, getting on with a wide range of people; secondly, I'm very well organised; and thirdly, I'm good at working on my own initiative. If I could just give a short example of each of these ...'

IN THE INTERVIEW

ANSWERING THE QUESTIONS

WEAKNESSES

'What weaknesses do you have?'

Pitfalls

The dangers here are:

1. Claiming you don't have any weaknesses (which will lead the interviewers to conclude that you are an egotist who lacks self-awareness)
2. Talking about a weakness that will worry them:

   'I'm hopeless at meeting deadlines.'

ANSWERING THE QUESTIONS

WEAKNESSES

'What weaknesses do you have?'

How to answer this question

- **Have two weaknesses** – When you've described your first weakness some panels will ask for another one, partly because they suspect that you have 'prepared' your first weakness especially for the interview.
- **Make sure they are things that won't worry the panel unduly** – Some weaknesses are more acceptable than others, depending on the job. A secretary can get away with saying, *'I sometimes find it hard to delegate; I often prefer to do things myself to make sure they get done the way I like'*. This obviously wouldn't be a good weakness for a managing director.
- **Talk about how you have worked on your weaknesses** to ensure that they don't become a problem. *'I work quite quickly, and sometimes I have a tendency to dive into tasks without taking a few moments to think things through. I've learned to discipline myself to spend a bit more time on planning, rather than constantly reacting to new demands on my time.'*

ANSWERING THE QUESTIONS

DIFFICULT COLLEAGUE

'How would you deal with a difficult colleague?'

Pitfalls

The pitfalls here are:

- Answering with a list of platitudes:

  'I think it's important to be nice and also fair with people. And communication is particularly important.'

- Giving a hypothetical answer:

  'Well, I would treat them fairly and try to understand why they were being difficult.'

ANSWERING THE QUESTIONS

DIFFICULT COLLEAGUE

'How would you deal with a difficult colleague?'

How to answer this question

Whenever you are faced with a question which is framed as *'how would you....'*, you should **answer with an example of how you have dealt with similar situations in the past.**

- **A real-life answer always sounds better** than a hypothetical view of what you might do – the latter can sound like you are simply parroting theories from training courses you have attended or books you have read.
- In this example you might say, *'Well, it would depend on the particular way in which they were being difficult. But, to choose one example, in my last job I worked with someone who could be very demanding and a bit unpredictable. I learned that the best way to deal with him was to invest a lot in the relationship so that we got on well most of the time, but also to stand up to him very assertively if I felt he was trying to take his frustrations out on me.'*

ANSWERING THE QUESTIONS

WHY THIS JOB?

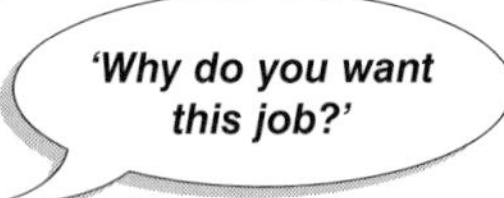

Pitfalls

Here you need to avoid giving a response which, though it might be one of the reasons why you are applying for a particular job, is not going to endear you to the interview panel.

You might want the job because:

- It is near to where you live
- You are fed up with your current boss
- You have been, or are about to be, sacked or made redundant

None of these reasons will impress the interview panel.

ANSWERING THE QUESTIONS

WHY THIS JOB?

'Why do you want this job?'

How to answer this question

- **Choose the reason most likely to appeal to the interview panel.** Enthusing about the shortness of your journey from home to work is unlikely to do this.
- Bear in mind that **joining an organisation is a bit like joining a family.** Your prospective manager is likely to be on the interview panel, and wants to hear that you are enthusiastic about working for them.
- This doesn't mean lying about why you are applying. **In reality, there is usually more than one reason for applying for a particular job.**
- **Focus on the reason that you know the panel will like.** You could talk about it being the kind of work you have had a lot of experience of and that you know you enjoy.

Top Tip – Show enthusiasm. The candidate with relevant experience, who is also enthusiastic, is a very appealing prospect. Sometimes enthusiasm will give you the edge over other equally well-qualified candidates.

QUESTIONS YOU SHOULD ASK

WHY ASK QUESTIONS?

'Surely I ask questions in the interview to get information about the job?'

No! Smart candidates recognise that the questions they ask are another opportunity for them to sell themselves and demonstrate why they are the best candidate.

When the panel says, usually towards the end of the interview, *'Do you have any questions for us?'* **the first thing to do is to gauge whether they actually have time for any.** They may be behind schedule with several more candidates to see. If it is clear from their body language and the way they ask the question that they are hoping you will say *'no'*, then it's probably best to say something like, *'No, I've had all my questions answered during the selection process, thank you'.*

If, however, you get the impression that they do have time for questions, there are three categories:

- **Bad Questions**
- **OK Questions**
- **Great Questions**

QUESTIONS YOU SHOULD ASK

BAD QUESTIONS

Bad questions tend to be questions that you really want the answer to. The problem is that they often don't present you in a very good light, and they never sell you. Examples of bad questions are:

'Do you operate a flexi-time system?'

'How much annual leave would I get?'

Candidates who ask these types of questions make employers nervous. They seem to be more interested in the perks than the job itself. Really weak candidates ask questions which show they haven't read the job pack properly.

QUESTIONS YOU SHOULD ASK

OK QUESTIONS

OK questions are also questions that you want the answers to. However, they will portray you in a better light than the bad questions.

Examples of OK questions are:

'What training and development opportunities are there within the organisation?'

'How long would I need to be in post before I would have the chance of promotion?'

There's nothing wrong with these questions in themselves, but there are better ones – questions which really impress the interview panel.

QUESTIONS YOU SHOULD ASK

GREAT QUESTIONS

Great questions are those that really sell you to the interviewers.

Great questions tell the panel something about you that they are going to like.

Great questions show that you have **initiative, drive and enthusiasm**.

'I've been thinking about some ways of marketing your product more effectively. I've used some of these methods in the past with good results – is there scope for new ideas like this within the department?'

'I've really enjoyed my experience of managing projects in my last job – would there be the opportunity for me to take on a specific project in this role?'

The secret of a great question is to have something to say about how you would perform in the job; then turn it into a question.

QUESTIONS YOU SHOULD ASK

WHY DO MY QUESTIONS MATTER?

- Your questions matter because they are often the last thing you say in an interview. **Just as your first impression counts, so does the image you leave with the interviewers.**
- If you settle for asking OK questions you run the risk of losing out to another candidate who asks great questions.

So, when do you ask the questions that you really want the answers to?

After they have offered you the job! At this stage you are no longer competing against the other candidates, so you no longer need to sell yourself. When you are offered the job, you can say something like:

'I'm delighted that you've offered me the job. Can I just check a couple of things about the terms and conditions.....'

NOT THE PERFECT CANDIDATE

THREE WAYS TO HANDLE THE SITUATION

Most candidates are not quite the ideal 'fit' for the job. It could be that you lack something that the employer has said that they want in prospective job holders, or it may be that there is something about your background or lifestyle that you know might put some employers off.

There are three ways to handle this:

1. **Don't volunteer information**

2. **If they know, or ask, have a good answer ready**

3. **Give them the answers to the questions they are afraid to ask**

NOT THE PERFECT CANDIDATE

THREE WAYS TO HANDLE THE SITUATION

1. Don't volunteer information

If the employer doesn't know about the problem area and doesn't ask, **it's generally not a good idea to volunteer information that you know they won't like.**

This is not dishonesty; it is a normal part of the mutual selling process that goes on in interviews. You can bet that the interviewers won't be telling candidates things about the organisation that they know will put them off.

NOT THE PERFECT CANDIDATE

THREE WAYS TO HANDLE THE SITUATION

2. If they know, or ask, have a good answer ready

Anticipate that the interviewers will want to ask about what they perceive as a weakness in your application, and have an answer ready.

If you are applying for a job with management responsibilities and you have no previous staff management experience you might say:

'I don't yet have any formal staff management experience; however I have developed all the skills needed by a staff manager.

For example, I have led groups of people in my voluntary work; I supervised temps in my last job and trained new staff. I've also learned how to deal assertively with colleagues and customers. On top of that, I have taken some short courses in how to manage staff.

So, although I have not had a formal staff management role, I have used all the skills needed of a manager.'

NOT THE PERFECT CANDIDATE

THREE WAYS TO HANDLE THE SITUATION

3. Give them the answers to the questions they are afraid to ask

There are some things about your background or experience that might worry some prospective employers.

Some employers are wary of offering a post to someone who is a single parent with young children. Their concern is that a single parent will have to leave early to pick up their children or will be prone to having days off at short notice to look after their sickly offspring.

Two things to bear in mind:

- It is unlawful for employers to discriminate against someone on the grounds of them being a parent
- If you are a parent you may not want to work for an employer that takes such a view

NOT THE PERFECT CANDIDATE

THREE WAYS TO HANDLE THE SITUATION

3. Give them the answers to the questions they are afraid to ask (cont'd)

Let's assume for a moment that you have young children and that the interviewers know this. You really want the job and you don't want them to be consciously or unconsciously influenced by the fact that you are a parent.

How do you handle this?

You find a way in the interview of talking about the brilliant childcare arrangements you have in place:

'One of the examples of my organisational skills is the way I have set up a really good system of childcare for my kids. I've managed to find a brilliant nursery that is very happy to look after my children when I work late. I'm also lucky in that my mum lives locally and will look after the children when they are ill.'

BLOWING YOUR OWN TRUMPET

The problem
Some interviewees find it difficult to sell themselves at interview for fear of coming across as boastful. They risk walking out at the end of the interview without having told the interview panel all the reasons why they are right for the job.

The solution
In practice, the problem can often be avoided by focusing on **examples** of what you have done rather than making **claims** about how great you are. Simply tell the panel about some of the challenges you have faced over the last few years and the things that went well, and let the evidence speak for itself. It helps if you can inject a bit of humour here too.

BLOWING YOUR OWN TRUMPET

EXAMPLE

Question
'Tell us about your strengths.'

Boastful answer
'I'm well organised and I'm a brilliant team player.'

Answer that sells you
'I believe that I am well organised – I have organised several large conferences at short notice and they all went very well. I would also say that I'm a good team worker – I really enjoy working with other people and my colleagues say that I'm good at keeping morale up. I have to say that I think the secret of this is my regular supply of tea and biscuits!'

FOUR THINGS TO AVOID

1. SAYING 'WE' INSTEAD OF 'I'

Our fear
Sometimes we say 'we' instead of 'I' when describing an achievement or the successful completion of a project because of a fear of sounding boastful.

The result
The downside of saying 'we' is that the interviewers wonder what your particular contribution was to the project or the achievement.

Remember that you and your achievements are the focus of the interview, so use 'I'.

FOUR THINGS TO AVOID

2. ARRIVING LATE

- This really irritates some interviewers – they often have a tight schedule for the day
- You may have been late for reasons totally outside your control, but the interviewers will still be irritated
- Allow plenty of time for your journey; if you are late apologise profusely, and make it clear that the reasons were things you couldn't possibly have foreseen

FOUR THINGS TO AVOID

3. LOOKING LIKE YOU WON'T FIT IN

It is amazing how even well-trained interviewers place a lot of emphasis on clothes and appearance, even if the way you dress would have no impact on your effectiveness in the job.

In some organisations the interview panel will take a dim view of tattoos and any kind of piercing other than earrings, and draw all sorts of unwarranted conclusions. In other organisations you may be marked down for lack of piercings!

In general, try and look like the people who work there already.

FOUR THINGS TO AVOID

4. BEING NEGATIVE

Being negative about anything can be a real turn-off for interviewers.

So, when they open the interview with, *'Was your journey OK?'* don't say, *'Well, actually no. The traffic was horrendous and finding somewhere to park was an absolute nightmare.'* This will create a bit of a heavy atmosphere right at the start.

Top Tip – It's even more essential to be positive about more important factors such as your relationship with your previous boss.

You may view your former manager as the boss from hell but the interviewers won't know him or her and may well view your negativity as disloyalty, or as evidence that you don't get on with managers generally.

THE PRESENTATION

OPPORTUNITY NOT THREAT

- Many interviews now include some kind of presentation from the candidate, often on a topic that will have been given to you in advance of the interview date.
- Most candidates dread the presentation part of the interview, **but if you prepare really well then this is a chance for you to shine** because it is the one part of the interview that you can control – you can plan and rehearse in advance exactly what you are going to say.
- Interviewers tend to be impressed by candidates who can deliver a confident, professional presentation, not least because many interviewers themselves find presentations daunting.

THE PRESENTATION

PREPARING

1. Make sure you know **what visual aids will be available within the room.** Will there be an overhead projector? a flip chart? data projector? laptop?

2. **Have a contingency plan** for when the equipment doesn't work. This usually means taking along paper copies of your slides – one for each interviewer. This is a nice touch even if the equipment works.

3. If you plan to use the flip chart, **take marker pens with you** – the ones in interview and training rooms are invariably at the end of their useful lives.

4. Make sure you understand exactly what the subject for the presentation is and how long you are expected to talk for.

THE PRESENTATION

PRACTISING

- Try not to rely on notes. Even if you have them to hand it is best if you can deliver your talk without referring to them. **If you have rehearsed enough, what you have to say will come out naturally and in a conversational style.** The more you rely on your notes, the more wooden you will appear.
- **Memorise your first line.** Many presenters lose their nerves once they are into their talk but find the first few moments very difficult. If you have memorised your first line and make a point of saying it confidently and not too fast it will ease you in.
- **Practise varying your voice by repeating a sentence in different ways** – emphasising different words and using different delivery styles and volume levels.

THE PRESENTATION

REHEARSING

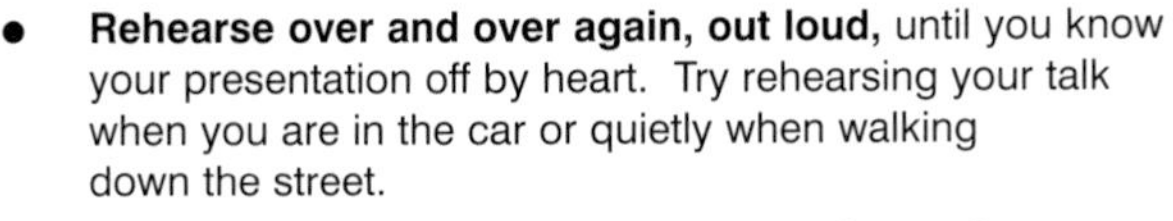

- **Rehearse over and over again, out loud,** until you know your presentation off by heart. Try rehearsing your talk when you are in the car or quietly when walking down the street.

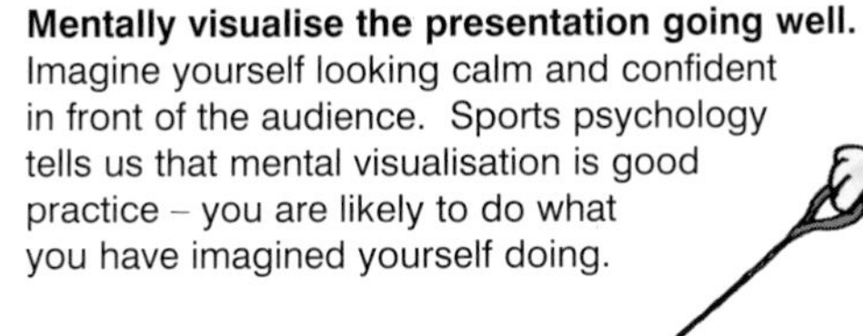

- **Mentally visualise the presentation going well.** Imagine yourself looking calm and confident in front of the audience. Sports psychology tells us that mental visualisation is good practice – you are likely to do what you have imagined yourself doing.

THE PRESENTATION

PUTTING YOUR POINTS OVER

- **When you stand up to speak, pause, take a deep breath and make eye contact with the interviewers.** It will seem like an eternity to you but only a moment to the panel and will prevent you from starting at a gallop.
- **Be positive, not a perfectionist.** Don't get steamed up about the fact that you might say *'um'* twice and forget a couple of points you wanted to make. Most of us do this and 99% of the time the interviewers don't notice.
- Remember to vary your tone during your talk – lots of presenters slip into a monotone. Change your pace, tone and volume during natural pauses (such as when you change a slide or start to make a new point). **It helps to think of your talk as a conversation rather than a presentation.**
- **Use short sharp phrases,** just as you would in a conversation. Avoid long rambling sentences which contain lots of sub clauses. These might be appropriate in a report but they are lifeless and difficult to follow in a presentation.

THE PRESENTATION

BODY LANGUAGE & GESTURES

Your body language when your make your presentation is just as important as in the question and answer part of the interview, and the same rules apply (eg, use your hands naturally).

Three things you should particularly remember to do in your presentation are:

1. **Stand, don't sit.** Research shows that presenters who stand are regarded by their audiences as being more credible and persuasive than those who deliver their talk sitting down.

2. **Stand equally balanced on both feet and feel the floor through the soles of your shoes.** Breathe from your abdomen. Try and relax into your body. A nervous presenter often loses touch with his/her body from the chest down, resulting in tense shoulders, shallow breathing and a strained sounding voice.

3. Make eye contact.

THE PRESENTATION

EYE CONTACT

When you make eye contact with the interviewers, what do you expect to see? Lots of nodding heads, smiles and interested looks? **Don't be put off by blank expressions.**

The reality is that many panels will stare back at you with blank faces or frowns. **This usually means they are listening to you – many people frown when concentrating** – so don't be disheartened if they don't look especially warm. Just as in the interview, avoid staring at one apparently friendly face.

THE PRESENTATION

USING VISUAL AIDS

Use visual aids wherever possible. There are four reasons for this:

1. People **remember more** if you show them images than if you simply tell them.

2. It is often **easier to understand** a point that is made visually.

3. Using slides or a flip chart **takes the focus off you** – this can be particularly welcome if you are feeling nervous.

4. If you are particularly nervous **your slides can remind you of what you want to say**, and if you really do stumble, at least your audience will pick up the gist of your message from your visuals.

IN THE INTERVIEW

THE PRESENTATION

DESIGNING SLIDES

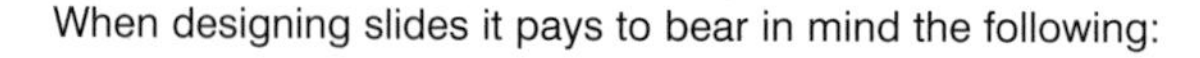

When designing slides it pays to bear in mind the following:

- **Big and bold is best.** Font size should be 16 point or larger. Use few words (5-6 words per line and 6-8 lines maximum). Don't use sentences.
- **Pictures are better than words.** In particular, graphs and charts are much easier to understand than tables of data.
- **If you can use colour, so much the better.** Well designed colour slides can look very professional and enhance your credibility.

ASSESSMENT CENTRES

INTRODUCTION

How assessment centres work
An assessment centre is basically a range of tests and exercises to assess your suitability for the job. Some organisations now use on-line ability or personality tests, which you can undertake from a computer at home without the need to attend a centre in person.

How long will it last?
If an organisation is using an assessment centre to select candidates they will need you to attend for anything between half a day and two days.

Why do organisations use them?
The organisation wants to see how you perform in a variety of settings and in the face of a range of challenges. An assessment centre allows them to test you more thoroughly than if they rely on an interview alone.

ASSESSMENT CENTRES

INTRODUCTION

What happens at an assessment centre?
In addition to interviews and presentations, assessment centres use a range of other tools to test you:

- Group exercises
- In-tray or case study exercises
- Psychometric tests
- Role plays
- Self-assessment

ASSESSMENT CENTRES

INTRODUCTION

TYPES OF EXERCISE

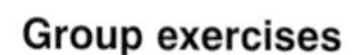

Group exercises
You are put in a group with other candidates and given a topic to discuss or a problem to solve. The assessors observe you during the exercise.

In-trays or case studies
In-trays are written exercises where you are given an in-tray full of letters, reports, email print-outs etc and asked to establish priorities and deal with them.
Case studies are written exercises where you are given a problem or a brief and asked to analyse it and come up with a recommendation.

Psychometric tests
Broadly, there are two types:

- **Ability tests**, which assess things such as your ability to work with figures. These are often multiple choice tests.
- **Personality tests**, which try to uncover what sort of person you are. These are also often multiple choice.

INTRODUCTION

TYPES OF EXERCISE

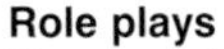

Role plays
You are asked to show in a role play how you would handle a particular situation; for example, dealing face-to-face with a complaint from a customer.

Self-assessment
You are asked to write an assessment of how you feel you have performed at the assessment centre.

INTRODUCTION

ABILITY TO PREDICT

Can these tools predict who will be good at the job? It depends. Some are quite good, some are hopeless.

Here's a summary of some of the different kinds of selection methods and how well they predict what the candidate will be like in the job. The correlation is the comparison between how well the candidate did in the assessment and how good they turned out to be in the job. A perfect correlation is 1.00.

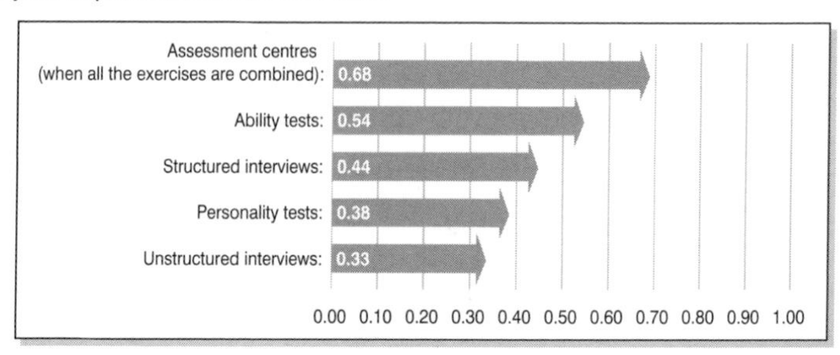

GROUP EXERCISES

WHAT THE ASSESSORS LOOK FOR

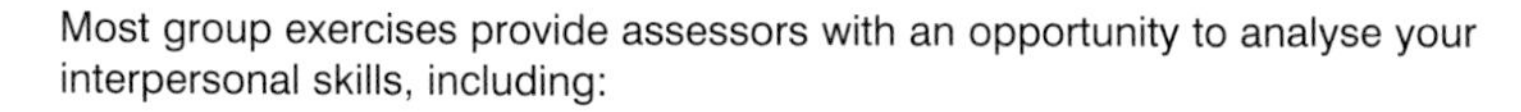
Most group exercises provide assessors with an opportunity to analyse your interpersonal skills, including:

- How you build relationships within a team
- The way that you communicate your ideas
- How well you listen to other members in the group
- Whether you can take the lead within the group
- Your leadership style when you do take the lead

The assessors may also be looking at your **problem solving skills** in the exercise.

GROUP EXERCISES

HOW TO IMPRESS THE ASSESSORS

Demonstrating good team skills

- **Build up good relationships** with the other people in your group during coffee breaks and meal times. This will mean they are more likely to listen to you in the group exercises.
- If you tend to be quiet in groups, **make sure you say something early on in the exercise** so you are 'included'.
- **Give the other group members 'positive strokes'** by praising their suggestions -- eg, *'that's a good idea'.*

GROUP EXERCISES

HOW TO IMPRESS THE ASSESSORS

Demonstrating good team skills (cont'd)

- **Demonstrate positive non-verbal behaviour.** This means giving the other group members lots of eye contact and nodding to show that you understand what they are saying. It also means limiting the amount of time you spend looking down at your notes or the exercise materials.
- **Consider taking on a particular role**, eg, time-keeper or note-taker – but be careful that the role doesn't hinder you from contributing more widely.
- **Strike a balance between advocacy and enquiry.** Advocacy is when you put forward your own views. Enquiry is when you ask other people about their ideas.

GROUP EXERCISES

HOW TO IMPRESS THE ASSESSORS

Showing leadership

- **Make suggestions about how the group should tackle the task** at the start of the exercise.
- **Chair the meeting.** You can either volunteer to do this at the start of the exercise, or simply adopt the role as it progresses.
- **Comment on how the group is working**, eg, *'We seem to be all talking at once. How about if we each take it in turns to put forward our suggestions?'*
- **Help to resolve conflicts within the group:** *'Jane, you're saying you don't like Mike's idea. Could you say what in particular you are unhappy about?'*

Top Tip – Don't get obsessed with the need to lead the group. It's only one of the qualities the assessors will be looking for. You don't have to lead for the whole of the exercise but **you should show some leadership at some point.**

IN-TRAYS OR CASE STUDIES

WHAT THE ASSESSORS LOOK FOR

- **The ability to pull out the key points from the material.** Often, the case study will contain lots of trivia and unimportant detail. Good candidates will be able to spot the important points.
- **Creativity** – the ability to come up with new perspectives and innovative ideas.
- **'Big picture' awareness** – taking a strategic view of the case study in terms of putting it in a wider context.
- **The ability to analyse** the data and draw conclusions.
- **Written communication skills** – being able to explain your analysis and recommendations. Some case studies will test your ability to write a tactful or diplomatic letter.
- **Clear action points** – many case studies require you to turn your analysis into an action plan.

IN-TRAYS OR CASE STUDIES

HOW TO IMPRESS THE ASSESSORS

What you write

- Ensure that you **answer all the questions** – you stand a much better chance of getting a good rating.
- Don't be afraid to **bring your own ideas** and any outside knowledge you have of the kind of scenarios described in the case study.
- Try not to get bogged down in detail. Often there is an overwhelming amount of information to analyse, so it's important that you **spot the key points and don't get distracted with more trivial factors.**
- **It's important to 'show your working'.** In other words, don't just set out your conclusions; explain the thinking behind them. Often there is no single 'right' answer to the case study – it's the quality of the analysis that the assessors are interested in.

IN-TRAYS OR CASE STUDIES

HOW TO IMPRESS THE ASSESSORS

How you write

- **Smart candidates use a structured approach to organise their thoughts.** One way of doing this is to construct a table with the advantages and disadvantages of each option.
- It's not always vital to have a finely polished written style, so long as your ideas are clearly set out. **Make sure you put plenty of structure in what you've written – use headings, subheadings and bulletpoints.**
- **One time when style does matter is if part of the case study requires you to write a letter or memo to one of the characters in the scenario.** This is usually a test to see if you can use language fluently and tactfully.
- If you are handwriting your answer, make sure your writing is legible. However, many organisations will provide you with a laptop computer for written exercises.

ABILITY TESTS

WHAT THE ASSESSORS LOOK FOR

There are many types of tests, and which one you encounter depends on the kind of job you go for. The most commonly used tests are:

- **Verbal reasoning** (which assess your command of English).
- **Numerical reasoning** (assessing your ability to use and interpret numbers). For many tests you are allowed to use a calculator (sometimes your own calculator). In these tests the assessors are more interested in your ability to interpret what the figures mean than in your ability to do accurate calculations.
- **IT aptitude** (testing your aptitude for IT related tasks such as computer programming).
- **Abstract logical thought** (which assess your general reasoning skills).

ABILITY TESTS

HOW TO IMPRESS THE ASSESSORS

Tactics

- **Make sure you know whether incorrect answers count against you.** Some tests deduct a mark for each incorrect answer. With these tests it's better not to guess at an answer. However, if a test does not deduct marks for incorrect answers you may as well guess.
- Try to work at a good pace. **Do a quick calculation at the start to work out how long you can afford to spend on each question.** If you get stuck on a question, move on to the next one. Don't forget to go back to the difficult questions when you have answered the easier ones.

ABILITY TESTS

HOW TO IMPRESS THE ASSESSORS

If you aren't good at tests

- **Don't be discouraged if you struggle** – these tests are designed to be hard. In some situations 10 correct answers out of 30 questions might be a good score. What counts is the 'comparison group' – ie, who the assessors are comparing you with.
- If you know, or suspect, that you have performed badly in one of the ability tests **it helps if you have something to say about this** if you are asked about it later in the assessment centre (eg, in an interview or as part of your self-assessment).

You might explain that you always have to allocate more time to figure work or that you sometimes ask for help from others. In other words, you need to show that you are aware of the weakness and are managing it.

PERSONALITY TESTS

TWO KEY POINTS

- Personality tests focus on **preferences rather than ability** – ie, what you enjoy doing rather than what you are good at. The rationale behind them is that we tend to be better in jobs that suit our preferences.

- **There is no ideal personality** that fits all jobs. The personality profile that the assessors are looking for varies hugely depending on the job.

PERSONALITY TESTS

WHAT THE ASSESSORS LOOK FOR

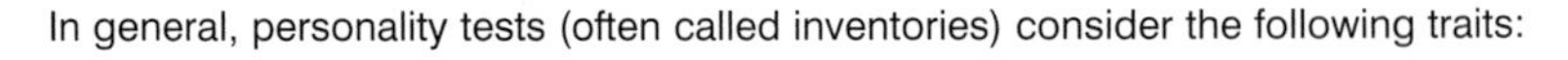
In general, personality tests (often called inventories) consider the following traits:

- How you prefer to relate to others, for example whether you like to work alone or as part of a team
- How motivated, competitive and driven you are
- How you handle stress
- Whether you enjoy leading other people
- Whether you enjoy the start-up phase of a project or prefer to be the person finishing things off
- Your levels of self-belief and confidence

PERSONALITY TESTS

HOW TO IMPRESS THE ASSESSORS

The trick, when completing personality tests, is:

Be your 'best self'

- By *best self* we mean how you are on a good day when you are on top form
- This is particularly important because sometimes when you are under pressure at an assessment centre you may not feel particularly confident, and this might influence the way you complete the personality inventory. So **adopt a positive frame of mind**
- Just like the ability tests, if you think there are aspects of your personality which may concern the assessors, it helps if you have a convincing explanation should they question you about these aspects later

PERSONALITY TESTS

HOW TO IMPRESS THE ASSESSORS

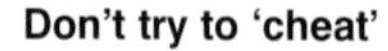

Don't try to 'cheat'

Don't try to paint a false picture of who you are when you complete the questionnaire. There are two reasons why doing this is a bad idea:

- Some tests have built-in checks to identify candidates who are attempting to portray an unduly rosy impression of themselves
- If your personality genuinely doesn't match the profile for the job, you probably wouldn't enjoy doing it anyway

ROLE PLAYS

WHAT THE ASSESSORS LOOK FOR

Role plays are often one-to-one exercises where the candidate has to deal effectively with someone playing the role of a difficult member of staff, a supplier or a customer. The other person may be an actor who has been hired for the assessment centre or someone from within the organisation.

Role plays are yet another way in which assessment centres test your communication skills. Role plays focus particularly on your:

- Assertiveness
- Listening skills
- Ability to negotiate

They also test your determination: can you continue to argue your case when the other person is resisting your views?

ROLE PLAYS

HOW TO IMPRESS THE ASSESSORS

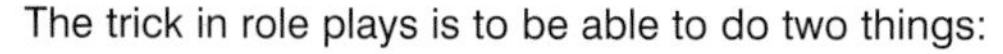

The trick in role plays is to be able to do two things:

1. **Stand up for your point of view**
2. **Build rapport with the other person and go for a collaborative approach to solving the problem**

Standing up for your point of view means knowing your 'bottom line' – which aspects of your case are you flexible about and which are non-negotiable?

Building rapport and collaborating with the other person means:

- Emphasising that you are working together to solve the problem: *'It sounds as though* **we** *need to....'* or: *'Let's talk about what options* **we** *might have...'*
- Really listening to their side of the story, and **showing** that you are listening: *'It sounds as though you are saying that....'*

Top Tip – If you are sitting down for the role play, avoid facing the other person directly. Research shows that sitting face-to-face for such conversations makes confrontation more likely. **Try to sit at right angles to the other person.**

SELF-ASSESSMENT

WHAT THE ASSESSORS LOOK FOR

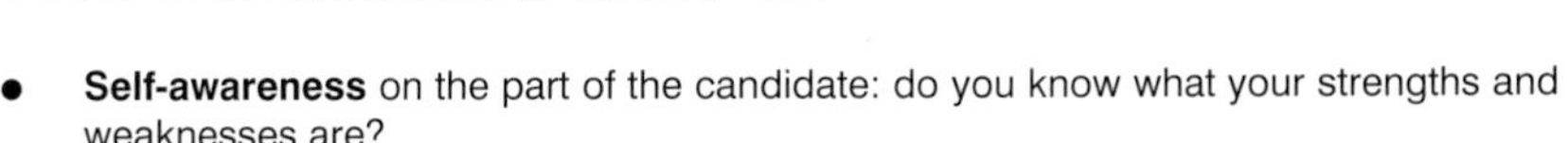

- **Self-awareness** on the part of the candidate: do you know what your strengths and weaknesses are?
- **Honesty about weaknesses.** You won't impress the assessors if you try to tell them that you don't have any weaknesses or development needs.
- **Insight into your performance so far at the assessment centre.** The assessors not only want to see that you are aware of how you have performed at the centre, they also want evidence that you have real insight into **why** you performed the way you did in the various exercises.
- **Clear and specific ideas** about what you can do to address your weaknesses and build on your strengths.
- **A positive attitude towards the assessment centre** (ie, don't blame the exercises or other candidates for any poor performance on your part).

SELF-ASSESSMENT

HOW TO IMPRESS THE ASSESSORS

- **Give an honest analysis** of how the assessment centre has gone for you so far.
- **Provide clear evidence of how you have developed in the past,** particularly in relation to past weaknesses. The assessors will want concrete evidence that you have done something about weaker areas in the past.
- **Be able to give the reasons behind the choices you made** in the various tests and the behaviours you showed in group exercises and role plays.
- **Be able to talk in detail about how you need to develop yourself** and what you plan to do about it.

AFTERWARDS

IF YOU ARE UNSUCCESSFUL

If you are unsuccessful, there are three things you need to do soon after the interview:

1. **Learn the lessons**
2. **Ask for feedback**
3. **Make sure you stay positive**

AFTERWARDS

IF YOU ARE UNSUCCESSFUL

1. LEARN THE LESSONS

This is partly about **getting feedback** and partly about **reflecting objectively on what you feel you did well in the interview, and what you should do differently next time.**

The trick here is to **focus on practical things you can do differently** rather than on aspects of yourself that you might not be able to change.

Resolving *'I will not be nervous next time'* is unlikely to be helpful as most people are nervous in interviews.

A better strategy would be to say to yourself, *'Next time I will remind myself just before the interview of all the reasons why I am a strong candidate, and I will also do some breathing exercises to help myself relax'.*

AFTERWARDS

IF YOU ARE UNSUCCESSFUL

2. ASK FOR FEEDBACK

Always, always, always, ask for feedback. You may feel disappointed after you receive the rejection letter and feel as though you never want to speak to the interviewers again, but getting feedback can give you invaluable information about the impression you create in interviews.

Ask for feedback even if you are offered the job. It shows you have a professional attitude and are always looking to improve. It also helps you to think about ways in which you might need to get up to speed before you start.

Talk to one of the interview panel – don't try and have the conversation with a member of the Human Resources Department who wasn't present in the interview.

IF YOU ARE UNSUCCESSFUL

2. ASK FOR FEEDBACK (Cont'd)

Have a list of questions you want to ask – they should focus on your performance rather than trying to get information about the other candidates and how you compared with them.

Be aware that many interviewers are wary about giving feedback. They worry that:

- They will hurt your feelings
- You will become defensive and argue
- You will use what they say to make a complaint

So you need to put reassure them when you telephone them to ask for feedback. Say something like: '*Thank you for inviting me for interview and I enjoyed meeting you, though I'm obviously disappointed that I wasn't successful on this occasion. I would really appreciate it if you could spare me 10 minutes to give me some feedback on how I might improve my chances at future interviews.*'

IF YOU ARE UNSUCCESSFUL

2. ASK FOR FEEDBACK (Cont'd)

How to handle the feedback

- Some interviewers will give you feedback too vague to be helpful. Eg: *'We thought you were good but another candidate had more relevant experience'.*
- You need more specific information than this. Questions you could ask are: *'What sort of experience do you think I need to make me a stronger candidate next time?'*

  'Was there anything about the way I answered the questions or presented myself during the interview that you think I need to consider changing in future?'

  'Can you remember what it was I did or said that created the impression that…'
- **During the conversation, say that you are finding the feedback helpful** – this will encourage them to say more.
- **Don't argue,** even if you don't agree. If you argue, the person giving the feedback is less likely to give you useful information. And they're not going to change their mind about their decision.
- Thank them.

IF YOU ARE UNSUCCESSFUL

3. STAY POSITIVE

Don't jump to conclusions

Sometimes after an unsuccessful interview, it is tempting to jump to an unhelpful conclusion about yourself and why you didn't get the job:

> *'I'm hopeless at interviews'*
> *'I don't have the experience employers are looking for'*

Think of all the possible explanations

Rather than jumping to an unhelpful conclusion, try to think of all the reasons why you might have been unsuccessful:

- There was another candidate who was exactly what they were looking for
- There were five other candidates; the odds were against you anyway
- Interviews are a lottery – the panel may have made a bad decision
- You didn't present yourself particularly well at that interview but you learned some useful lessons for future interviews

STAYING POSITIVE

WHAT ARE YOU FEELING BAD ABOUT?

Sometimes an unsuccessful interview or other disappointing experience leaves us feeling disproportionately gloomy. **This can be because we have made some depressing assumptions about what being unsuccessful at an interview means.** We don't always realise what sort of assumptions and beliefs have crept into our minds:

'I'll never get another job' *'I'm a failure professionally'*

One way to feel more cheerful is to examine the conclusion you have come to. Work through these questions:

1. What is the thought or belief that is making me feel gloomy?
2. What evidence supports my thought or belief?
3. What evidence is against this thought or belief?
4. Is there an alternative explanation?
5. What is the worst that could happen? Could I live through it?
6. What is the best that could happen?
7. What is the most realistic outcome?
8. What is the effect of my holding this belief or dwelling on this thought?
9. What would be the effect of changing my thinking?
10. What thought or belief would be more helpful to me?

AFTERWARDS

STAYING POSITIVE

CHOOSE TO BE OPTIMISTIC

Optimists tend to look on the bright side; pessimists focus on the negatives.

There is evidence to suggest that optimists:

- Are happier
- Live longer
- Are more successful

AFTERWARDS

STAYING POSITIVE

HOW TO BE A PESSIMIST

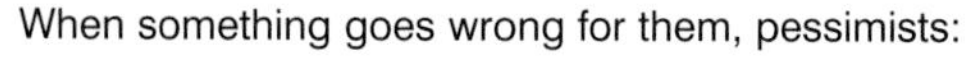

When something goes wrong for them, pessimists:

- Blame themselves – *'They didn't offer me the job because I performed badly at interview'*
- Think things will continue to go badly for them – *'I'm not good at interviews; I'll have the same problems at the next one'*
- Generalise into other areas of their lives – *'This is typical of me: I'm useless when I have to meet new people'*

However when things go well for them, pessimists:

- Don't give themselves credit – *'I don't know why they offered me the job – maybe they didn't interview anyone else'*
- Think this is a one-off stroke of good fortune – *'I was lucky this time, but I bet they'll find me out'*
- See this positive experience as not typical of their lives – *'This interview went well, but I know that I'm not good at meeting new people'*

AFTERWARDS

STAYING POSITIVE

HOW TO BE AN OPTIMIST

When something goes wrong for them, optimists:

- Avoid blaming themselves – *'Maybe they didn't offer me the job because they already had an internal candidate lined up'*
- See this as a one-off occurrence – *'I usually do well at interviews; I'm sure things will go better next time'*
- Avoid generalising into other areas of their lives – *'This was just one job interview; I know that I have good communication skills generally'*

However when things go well for them, optimists:

- Give themselves credit – *'I'm good at presenting myself at interview and I know I'll be good in the job'*
- Expect other good things to happen in future – *'It's good to know that if this job doesn't work out I'll be able to find another one easily'*
- See this positive experience as typical of their lives – *'I know that I have good communication skills and enjoy meeting people, so interviews generally go well for me'*

TEN TIPS TO TAKE AWAY

1. Remember that the job goes to the candidate who performs best on the day of the interview: preparation is vital
2. When you're preparing for the interview, gather 'intelligence' in addition to the information the organisation sends you
3. Rehearse stories and examples that illustrate your strengths
4. Dress to fit in, and make sure you're comfortable in your clothes
5. Do a 'dummy run' of your journey to the interview venue so that you arrive on time
6. Use breathing exercises to control your nerves
7. When you walk into the interview room smile, make eye contact and shake hands
8. Sit with a confident posture, then be yourself
9. Ask great questions which sell you
10. Ask for feedback after the interview

About the Author

Peter English

Peter has more than twelve years experience in management and organisational development. For the past seven years he has run his own consultancy practice and during this time he has trained hundreds of managers in how to use the latest selection techniques when recruiting people to their organisations. He has also managed large scale recruitment campaigns for a major UK employer.

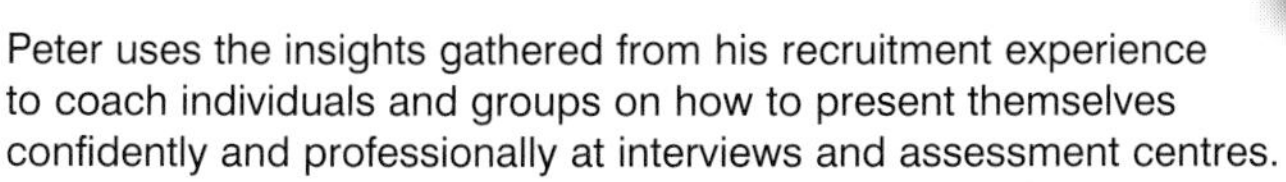

Peter uses the insights gathered from his recruitment experience to coach individuals and groups on how to present themselves confidently and professionally at interviews and assessment centres.

Contact

He can be contacted by email at
pete@peterenglish.co.uk

ORDER FORM

Your details

Name ______________________

Position ______________________

Company ______________________

Address ______________________

____

____

Telephone ______________________

Fax ______________________

E-mail ______________________

VAT No. (EC companies) ______________________

Your Order Ref ______________________

Please send me:

			No. copies
The	Succeeding at Interviews	Pocketbook	
The		Pocketbook	
The		Pocketbook	
The		Pocketbook	
The		Pocketbook	

Order by Post

MANAGEMENT POCKETBOOKS LTD

LAUREL HOUSE, STATION APPROACH,
ALRESFORD, HAMPSHIRE SO24 9JH UK

Order by Phone, Fax or Internet

Telephone: +44 (0)1962 735573
Facsimile: +44 (0)1962 733637
E-mail: sales@pocketbook.co.uk
Web: www.pocketbook.co.uk

MANAGEMENT POCKETBOOKS